Nabakalebara

Nabakalebara

Sankar Prasad Tripathy

Translated by
Sanjeet Kumar Das

BLACK EAGLE BOOKS
Dublin, USA | Bhubaneswar, India

Black Eagle Books
USA address:
7464 Wisdom Lane
Dublin, OH 43016

India address:
E/312, Trident Galaxy, Kalinga Nagar,
Bhubaneswar-751003, Odisha, India

E-mail: info@blackeaglebooks.org
Website: www.blackeaglebooks.org

First International Edition Published by
Black Eagle Books, 2024

NABAKALEBARA
by **Sankar Prasad Tripathy**

Translated by **Sanjeet Kumar Das**

Original Copyright © Sankar Prasad Tripathy
Translation Copyright © Sanjeet Kumar Das

All rights reserved. No part of this publication may be reproduced, stored in a retrieval system, or transmitted, in any form or by any means, electronic, mechanical, photocopying, recording or otherwise without the prior permission of the publisher.

Cover & Interior Design: Ezy's Publication

ISBN- 978-1-64560-515-7 (Paperback)
Library of Congress Control Number: 2024931830

Printed in the United States of America

For
Swopna, my daughter
Sujata, my wife
and
Bapa and Maa

Author's View

Jagannatha is the Supreme Consciousness, above all consciousness. He is eternal. The human sense of values flows sweetly in perennial streams to this great courtyard of the Jagannatha Cult. The sense of values that remains unaltered for ages is what the Jagannatha Culture is all about.

Brahma (Supreme Soul) can't be destroyed by any means. The play *Nabakalebar* focuses on the oneness and the universality of it. The good always wins over the evil. The people on the path of righteousness are divinely blessed and at last, victory comes to them.

"nainaṃ chindati śastrāṇi nainaṃ dahati pāvakḥ
na cainaṃ kledayantyāpo na śoṣayati mārutaḥ"

"Weapons cleave It not, fire burns It not, water moistens It not, wind dries It not."

Shankar Prasad Tripathy

Translator's View

One of the renowned playwrights of Odisha, Shankar Prasad Tripathy's *Nabakalebara* is a historical play. The Jagannath culture is so vast that all other cultures can confluence in its perennial streams of human values. Its universality and all-embracing approach appeal to people worldwide forever. 'Why we celebrate Nabakalebar' is foregrounded and well-substantiated thematically in the play. The ideas mapped in this work of art can be critically analyzed as follows: (1) the human desire for territorial expansion as in the character of Akbar, the Great and Mukunda Deva, to some extent because of his alliance with Rudranarayan of Bhurishrestha of the 'Land of Banga' to fight against Suleiman Karrani, the King of 'Gouda Land' (2) The primal instinct of love obliterating social boundaries persists between Kalapahada, commander-in-Chief of the combined force of the King of Kalinga and Bhurishrestha and Gulnaz, the daughter of Suleiman Karrani, of 'Land of Gouda' (3) the traumatic experiences of the protagonist lacking spiritual bliss, after fulfilling his love-marriage with Gulnaz and his subsequent revengeful acts against the deities and the people of Odisha, (4) Reinstallation of

Brahmas in the idols and their mounting on the bejewelled throne (*Ratnasinghashana*) at the Jagannatha Temple, Puri reaffirms and rejuvenates faith in the people again that Brahma (Supreme Soul) is One and only One, eternal and can't be destroyed by anybody and anything in the material world. That's why, Kalapahada, at last broke apart, while trying to burn it in fire. Jagannatha is the root cause of everything happening in the world. His blessing helps the people move forward in day-to-day life.

The *Nabakalebara* festival is deeply rooted in the psyches of the people who love the Jagannatha cult. It's similar to the demise and rebirth of life in all religions of the world. It happens every twelve years. Anything that comes out of this earth is subject to decay and change. The external bodily forms of the idols are buried under the soil in *Koilibaikuntha*, Puri, whereas the Brahma remains intact and installed again in the newly made wooden idols. There is one and only one Brahma in the world. That can't be drowned in water, burnt in fire; that can't be severed or split and will remain unaltered for ages. Once the idols are half-burnt and thrown into the sea, they can't be worshipped. The new idols (*Darubrahmas*) are installed and mounted on the (*Ratnasinghasana*) bejewelled throne at Jagannatha Temple, Puri. Selection of *Darus* as per the order of Goddess Mangala, and its felling after chanting the mantras, and performing *Yajna*, transferring the *Darus* loaded on bullock carts to Jagannatha Temple, Puri, and replacing older idols by the newer ones, and lastly installing Brahmas in the newer *Darus* are the processes related to *Nabakalebara* ceremony.

Yaduvanshi Bhoi King Ramachandra Deva organized the First Nabakalebar in 1575 A.D. It commemorates the symbolic death and resurrection of Jagannath at Puri. At one point, General Kalapahad of the Bengal Sultan attacked the Jagannath Temple in Puri and removed the idol of Lord Jagannath to demolish it. He discovered the idol's Daru Brahma portion was challenging when he attempted to burn it. He dumped the remainder into the Ganga River. Following Kalapahad with the idol from Orissa to Bengal, the Bisara Mohanty floated down the stream and saved the Daru Brahma. He concealed it in a mridangam (drum) and carried it covertly to his Kujang village. There, he had made modest sacrifices to the Daru Brahma in adoration. In a dream, Lord Jagannath gave a command to the new monarch, Ramachandra Deva. After renovations, King Ramachandra installed the idols in the Jagannath temple in Puri. He gave Bisara Mohanty the title of Nayaka (chief) of the Purushottama Kshetra, acknowledging his participation in the organization.

I have tried my best to keep the language as lucid as possible. While following the rules of equivalence and the rules of faithfulness between the Odia language and the English language, I came across some natural shifts. However, I have retained the culture-specific terms of the Jagannatha Cult of Odisha as they are, while translating from Odia into English. I agree with Lawrence Venuti's concept of 'Foreignization' while translating the original Odia text. A list of words is incorporated with my translation as a glossary. It will help the readers understand and maintain the flow of thoughts successively.

First, I thank Sankar Prasad Tripathy for having faith in me to translate his text carefully. I convey my gratitude to Dr. Pradosh Kumar Swain, Assistant Professor, Central University of Odisha, for helping me select this text for the stuff of my work. I am grateful to Dr Manoj Kumar Tula, faculty, Central University of Odisha, for editing the text and Dr Niladrinath Das, retired Professor of English, Vikramdev University, Jeypore, Koraput, for his critical insights.

I convey my heartfelt gratitude to Sri Satya Pattanaik, the director of Black Eagle Books, USA and Sri Ashok Parida of the publishing house for their kind consent to publish the texts in time.

Sanjeet Kumar Das

Critic's View

English Translation of Sankar Prasad Tripathy's *Nabakalabara* by Sanjeet Kumar Das is the outcome of his diligent endeavour and scholastic effort in the field of Oriental Mysticism on cosmic energy or God.

The philosophy of the Jagannath cult is based on the Oriental Metaphysics of Creation Theory. Vedantic Philosophy accepts the concept of duality, where Creation is nothing but an illusion; where the divine spirit manifests itself in the form of matter. Vedantic Philosophy speaks on three essential elements of the Creation: Supreme Soul (Brahma), Illusion (Maya), and God (Ishwara). These three forces represent Jagannatha, Subhaddra and Balabhadra respectively.

Nabakalebara is based on the philosophy of Purusha (Soul) and Prakriti (Body). It is a synthesis of the Dravidian culture of idol-making and Aryan rituals. Besides these, we find a mélange of philosophical or metaphysical theories. Thus, the Bramha (Supreme Consciousness) is eternal, while the tangible *Daru* is subject to transformation as has been mentioned in the Bhagwat Gita:

"*vāsāṁsi jīrṇāni yathā vihāya
navāni gṛhṇāti naroparāṇi
tathā sarīrāṇi vihāya jīrṇā-
anyāni saṁyāti navāni dehī*"

As we get rid of our old clothes with a new one, in the same way, this soul (Atma) gives up the old body and dwells in a new one.

Nabakalebara, on the philosophical plain is the demonstrative *Purusha* and *Prakriti*. Thus, *Bramha* is incorporated into the new body at regular intervals.

The tradition of *Nabakalebara* is both philosophical and cultural. Here, God is also subjected to His divine principles. Thus, *Nabakalebara* is one of the principal components of the Jagannath cult. Regarding the installation of *Bramha*, we have synergistic theories of *Salagram*, holy Relics of Lord Krishna or Lord Buddha and the sacred remains of the Primordial Idol built by Indradyumna. In any case, *Darubramha* is the manifestation of eternal *Bramha* or the Supreme Energy.

Dr. Niladrinath Das
Retired Professor of English
Department of English
Vikramdev University, Jeypore, Koraput

Nabakalebara

A significant ritual, the *Nabakalebara*, is associated with the worship of Lord Jagannath in Odisha, India. It revolves around the religious beliefs and cultural practices of the Odia people. Anthropologically, it is very significant and unique because of its social, cultural, and symbolic dimensions; if we look at the history of human civilization since evolved in the human mind, that unique quality of consciousness, reflective self-awareness, origin myths such as the concept of ancestral worship, rebirth, reincarnation, etc., has been central to the intellectual lives of modern man everywhere. Like every human society and culture, Odia culture has its version of the "Origin Myth" of *Nabakalebara*, where myth is used as an allegory. The product of the unique curiosity of the human mind, origin myths nevertheless tell how a particular community might have experienced there. They encompass a worldview that enunciates how people should behave nowadays. Origin myths in Odia culture are prescriptive, not just descriptive. They present a microcosm of Odia society, of how people behave with each other, how men live with women, how "native people" relate with "outsiders," and of the place of humans in the world of nature. It has been evidenced that the people in Odisha embrace different stocks of people diachronically in acculturation.

The geographical boundary of the State of Odisha was never fixed in history. Historical evidence also reveals that the ancient geography of Odisha is traced through various names, such as Kalinga, Utkal, Odra, Tosali and Kosal and is mentioned in the mythologies of the ancient Sanskrit and Pali literature. In Odisha, the recent archaeological excavations, linguistic evidences, and findings on human molecular genetics give new insights into the Neolithic Chalcolithic cultural tradition and possible early urbanization in coastal Odisha, occupation of the land, and different waves of migration. Evidence from various sources, such as the presence of Austro-Asiatic linguistic groups with Neolithic-shouldered axes, agriculture, domestication of plants and animals and different cultural practices in Odisha, has its tribal roots. Similarly, in every sphere of life of Odia people, the reflection of their evolutionary past manifested. Mainly, when we look at Jagannath Culture, central to Odia people's way of living, its roots are still observed among the *Soura* and *Kondha* tribal communities despite many acculturations. We can't understand Odisha's political economy for better governance and administration without understanding how Odia people situate themselves in this natural world and not in the light of scientific justifications, which are often rejected, but by imbibing the origin, which is profoundly reflected in the day to day activities of the Odia people. Therefore, if we trace the origin of *Nabakalebara*, we have to understand the protagonist *Kalapahada* and his strong inclination towards his roots.

Kanhu Charan Satapathy
Associate Professor, Department of Anthropology
Utkal University, Bhubaneswar, Odisha

Dramatis Personae

Padmavati
Gulnaz
Mukunda Deva
Durga Bhanja
Ramachandra Deva
Ramachandra Bhanja
Rudra Narayan
Suleiman Karrani
Kalapahada
Rajguru
Dana Patra
Bishar Mohanty
Umrao
Old Woman
Messenger
Spy
Servitor-I
Servitor-II
Servitor-III
Servitor-IV
Servitor-V

SCENE-I

['Jay Jagannatha' is heard from the camp at 'Land of Banga'. Subsequently, 'Let there be victory for Gajapati Mukunda Deva' is heard. After the stage light, Mukunda Deva and Rudranarayan are seen standing on the stage.]

Rudranarayan : The King of Bhurishrestha, Rudranarayan, welcomes Gajapati Mukunda Deva of Odisha. Our friendship has disturbed Nawab Suleiman Karrani of the 'Land of Gouda' nowadays.

Mukunda Deva: Our friendship is not the only reason of Suleiman Karrani's annoyance. My relationship with Mughal Emperor Akbar matters. Akbar, the Great wants the end of Afghan rule in Bengal. So, when I allowed Ibrahim to shelter at my palace, Suleiman showed his annoyance at the intimacy.

Rudranarayan : Why do you worry about that?

Mukunda Deva: If not today, tomorrow Suleiman will invade Kalinga. But before that, we must

	defeat the Afghans and restrict their power to the 'Land of Banga'.
Rudranarayan :	The Army of Bhurishrestha is always ready for that. Though I won't surrender to Akbar, Suleiman is my enemy. By hook or by crook, the enemies are to be conquered and controlled.
Mukunda Deva:	My dear Rudranarayan! The ruler of Kalinga is Lord Jagannatha Himself. I am his servitor. One who eyes Kalinga develops a sense of betrayal with Lord Jagannatha, and he can't be forgiven. We have to preserve Kalinga's pride for Jagannatha.

[In the second stage are Suleiman Karrani and Ramachandra Bhanja.]

Suleiman	: Jagannatha, Jagannatha, Jagannatha! Ramachandra! Please tell me what Jagannatha is and how he is.
Ramachandra :	Jagannatha is the Greatest Emperor of Odisha.
Suleiman	: (Laughing) The Emperor! With this comment, how come an ordinary piece of wood can elevate my mind to the sky's height? It has the courage and conviction to defeat the Mughals and Afghans. But I am the enemy of Hindus, Suleiman Karrani. I will completely ruin the 'Pride of Odisha' Jagannatha by invading the 'Land of this Race'.

[On the first stage, Mukunda Deva and Rudranarayan are

discussing near the camp.]

Mukunda Deva: (Laughing) Nobody is born in this world so far to destroy Lord Jagannatha. Jagannatha is the Ultimate Truth and the Supreme Bhagabata. He is the Supreme Consciousness, above all consciousness. He is eternal. The human sense of values flow sweetly in perennial streams to this great courtyard of Jagannatha Cult; the sense of values that remains unaltered for ages is what the Jagannatha Culture is all about.

Rudranarayan : Let the preparation be made for invasion!

Mukunda Deva: But who will be the General of both Kalinga and Bhurishrestha's Army?

Rudranarayan : My General Kalapahada!

Mukunda Deva: Kalapahada!

[Kalapahad enters.]

Kalapahada : I say 'pranam' to Gajapati of Kalinga, Mukunda Dev, and the King of Bhurishrestha, Rudra Narayan.

Mukunda Deva: Kalapahada! You have been assigned the responsibility of Chief Commander of both the Armies. We are sure that you can resist and defeat the Army of Suleiman Karrani courageously and easily.

Kalapahada : I promise you won't find any trace of an Afghan on the 'Land of Banga'.

[Mukunda Deva and Rudranarayan have put their hands on Kalapahada's shoulder.]

[Light off]

SCENE-II

[It's the battlefield: on one side, Suleiman Karrani and his army and on the other side, Kalapahada, Mukunda Deva, and Rudranarayan, along with their army.]

Suleiman : Mukunda Deva! You have declared an adventurous fight with the 'Nawab of Gouda'. You will face its consequences.
Mukunda Deva: The result of the battle will decide who has made a mistake.
Kalapahada : Before you reach Kalinga's Gajapati, you first face Kalapahada in battle, the 'Nawab of Gouda'! I have promised that neither the Mughals nor the Afghans can reach the 'Land of Banga'. Let the army proceed to attack!
Suleiman : Counterattack them!

[Battle continues between them. Suleiman Karrani is vanquished and leaves the battlefield.]

Mukunda Deva : I have been pleased with your bravery. I now hand over to you the responsibility of my Saptagram in the 'Land of Banga'.

Rudranarayan : Suleiman Karrani has been defeated in the fight. So, he is compelled to sign a treaty with us. We will forcefully occupy the 'Land of Gouda', if he hesitates to sign.
Mukunda Deva: Kalapahada! I am sure he will sign if you proceed to Suleiman with a treaty proposal. We will take necessary actions against him if he doesn't sign.
Kalapahada : As you wish, Maharaja!

[Light off]

SCENE-III

[Suleiman Karrani and Ramachandra Bhanja talk to each other.]

Suleiman : I have exercised my authority over the 'Land of Banga'. But Mukunda Deva defeated me in the battle. I can't forget this insult, Ramachandra Bhanja! I will take revenge against him.

Ramachandra : If Mukunda Deva makes an alliance with Rudranarayan for his self-interest, why can't the King of Saranga Gada be a friend to you against Kalinga?

Suleiman : If you join your hands only, you won't succeed. Their strength is Kalapahada. Until Kalapahada deserts them, fighting against Bhurishrestha and the Army of Kalinga will be in vain.

Ramachandra : You think of Bhurishrestha only. Nowadays, conspiracies are already plotted in the surroundings of the Kalinga Throne. That one kills another for the post of Gajapati is the duty of a king.

Suleiman : What are you talking nonsense?

Ramachandra : It's meaningful. It's the truth. Having

	killed eighteen sons of Prataprudra Deva, Chief Commander Govinda Bidyadhar became Utkal's Gajapati. This Mukunda Harichandan is Govinda Bidyadhar's friend. Narasingh Jena murdered Bidyadhar's son, Chakra Pratap. Again Mukunda Harichandan, having killed Narasingh Jena, entered Barabati Fort. All the Commanders-in-Chief of the regiments of Kalinga are with me. If you support us, we can occupy the Kalinga Throne.
Suleiman	: Well, this is right. But I need Kalapahada.

[At this time, the messenger steps in with a message.]

Messenger	: Someone has come to meet you, Nawab.
Suleiman	: Who is there? What's his name?
Messenger	: I have never seen him earlier. When I asked, he said 'his name is Kalapahada'.
Suleiman	: What you say! Kalapahada has come! And now the camel is under the mountain. Go and send him here immediately. Ramachandra, you go inside!

[Messenger and Ramachandra leave the spot.]

Suleiman	: I can't believe Kalapahada will come to me so early. Why has he come? What is his purpose of visit?
	[Kalapahada enters.]
Kalapahada	: I salute the 'Nawab of Gouda' Suleiman Karrani!

Suleiman	: Kalapahada, you come. I am thrilled to meet you today. You are indeed a warrior. I have never seen a warrior like you in this 'Land of Banga'. If Rudranarayan and Mukunda Deva won the battle, it would have been possible only because of your strength and bravery. Please tell me the reason of your visit.
Kalapahada	: On behalf of Kalinga and Bhurishrestha, I have sent you the 'Proposal for Peace'.
Suleiman	: I have already accepted this proposal earlier. Apart from that, when you come here with the proposal, it means a lot to me.
Kalapahada	: It gives me immense pleasure that you have accepted our proposal. I have heard a lot about you, but I have been changed after I meet you.
Suleiman	: What have you heard about me?
Kalapahada	: You are a dictatorial Nawab (ruler). You hate the Hindus.
Suleiman	: What you have heard about me is correct. Each Nawab wants his territorial expansion. I don't have hatred for the Hindus, but for Delhi's emperor Akbar, who wants the Mughal Empire to expand all over the country.
Kalapahada	: This is a good idea!
Suleiman	: But your King Mukunda Deva has already surrendered before Akbar. Anyway, we will discuss it later. Today, you are our guest. It's my responsibility to honour you. Gulnaz!

[Suleiman calls and Gulnaz comes in.]

Gulnaz	:	Have you called me, *Abbajan*?
Suleiman	:	This is Kalapahada. He is the General of the Combined Army of Bhurishrestha and Kalinga. From today onwards, he will be our guest. I have assigned you the responsibility to look after him.
Gulnaz	:	Your guest won't face any problems, *Abbajan*! (Suleiman leaves.) Why do you look at me?
Kalapahada	:	Are you Gulnaz?
Gulnaz	:	Yes!
Kalapahada	:	Very good… (Gulnaz smiles, and Kalapahada looks at her.) A beautiful rose, whose name is Gulnaz, has blossomed in Nawab Suleiman Karrani's garden. Are you a human or an angel?
Gulnaz	:	(smiling) Haven't you seen earlier?
Kalapahada	:	How can I get that opportunity? Had I seen, the flower would have blossomed at Kalapahada's house instead of Nawab's garden.
Gulnaz	:	I have heard that you are a warrior. Can you train me in archery?
Kalapahada	:	The arrows of your eyes have already bruised my heart. How will I train you?
Gulnaz	:	Stop joking. Please tell me whether you will teach me or not.
Kalapahada	:	I grant your wish!
Gulnaz	:	Abbajan has assigned me your hospitality. He will be angry if I commit any negligence in my duty. Please do come to our Guest House.
Kalapahada	:	Everything will be available at Nawab's

Guest House. I don't need all those, but I need Gulnaz's love. Can you approve?

[Gulnaz leaves the place smiling. Kalapahada stands there.]

[Light off]

SCENE-IV

[Durga Bhanja stands inside the Barabati Fort. The Messenger declares.]

Messenger : The Maharani Padmavati returns from the *Gahana Bije* (The Queen's visit to Jagannatha's Temple, Puri with enough security system in the city). Be alert.

[Padmavati comes with Chhatritras in a paliquin and gets down.]

Padmavati : Have you heard, General, that Gajapati Maharaj has won the battle against the Nawab of Gouda? I visited Jagannatha Temple on *Gahana Bije* for that.

Durgabhanja : Yes, Maharani. There was hostility between Gouda Nawab and Gajapati for a long time. Having been defeated in Delhi, the Nawab Ibrahim Khan reached the 'Land of Banga'. Suleiman Karrani thought of him as his enemy and tried to arrest him. Then, he took shelter in Kalinga. That's why there was an intense rivalry between Gajapati Mukunda Deva

	and Gouda Nawab for long. Everything comes to an end after this battle.
Padmavati	: That's not all. To dethrone your Gajapati from power, the Muslims of the 'Land of Banga' helped our baron King Raghu Bhanja fight. But at last, they got defeated.

[The Messenger announces at this time.]

Messenger	: *Virashree Gajapati Goudeshwar, Nabakoti Karnat Kalabargeswar Viradhi Virabar* Sri Sri Sri Mukunda Devaray enters.

[Mukunda Deva enters.]

Durgabhanja	: I congratulate you, Gajapati, for winning over the 'Land of Gouda'.

[One brings on a plate some flowers, rice and a lamp. Padmavati waves the light. Then the man returns with the plate.]

Padmavati	: Congratulations to you for the victory of the 'Land of Gouda'!
Mukunda Deva:	It's not my victory. It's the victory of Lord Jagannatha. Because of the Kalinga's Gajapatis, no Mughal or Afghan has dared to enter Kalinga so far. The Gajapatis of Kalinga faced Emperor Akbar's 'Territorial Expansion Rules' on the one hand, while on the other hand, the greed of the Afghan Rulers in the 'Land of Banga' to have victory over Kalinga. Because of our faith in Lord Jagannatha, external enemies or outsiders have not successfully invaded Kalinga.
Padmavati	: Why do you talk of only the external enemies? A good number of enemies

hide inside the state of Kalinga, too. Some days earlier Raghubhanja also fought against you. Sarangagada's King Ramachandra Bhanja has maintained a good relationship with Suleiman Karrani.

Mukunda Deva: I know that story, Maharani! Those who stay inside the glass house and pelt stones at the houses built up of rocks suffer a lot. That has already been proved in the defeat of Suleiman Karrani.

Durgabhanja: Still, we have to be vigilant and aware of the enemies inside the state. Ramachandra betrays us. Why don't you punish him after knowing all this?

Mukunda Deva: In politics, enemies and friends are treated equally. Let Ramachandra Bhanja plot the conspiracies against us. One day, he will be trapped in the conspiracy he plotted.

Durgabhanja : I can't accept the decision you are taking now, Gajapati!

Mukunda Deva: The General! You remember, Lord Jagannatha decides who will be the Gajapati to the 'Throne of Kalinga'. It is because Gajapati is the first servant to Lord Jagannatha. Time will determine whether Ramachandra Bhanja or I will win the conspiracy plotted against the 'Throne of Kalinga'. Let us celebrate together our victory.

[Light off]

SCENE-V

[Gulnaz waits for Kalapahad, holding a bow in her hands. Kalapahada has reached there. Gulnaz shows her irritation.]

Gulnaz	:	Where were you so long?
Kalapahada	:	I had a work with your father.
Gulnaz	:	You know that I don't like to stay alone.
Kalapahada	:	Then, you allow me to stay with you every day!
Gulnaz	:	I also want that. Please come and teach me how to learn the art of archery.

[Kalapahada trains Gulnaz the archery in different poses. While training, he embraces her in one hand.]

Boy	:	The sparkle in your eyes, your naughty look lights a thousand lamps in my heart.
Girl	:	In the lamp's flame is written today that love is a holy sin.
Boy	:	For that, only my mind searches for you day and night and your love has sweetly scandalized me.
Boy	:	I swear to God.
Girl	:	I swear to God.

Boy	:	I am unruly now; I am bruised in love, my female companion.
Girl	:	The clever hunter aiming at the goalpost has shot the arrow of flower. (The arrows of Cupid strike both the hearts of man and woman in Love.)
Boy	:	I have sacrificed my life for your love's kindness.
Girl	:	If you have come into my life, never will you desert me.
Boy	:	For my love-struck heart, your love is Muharram.
Girl	:	Hey, your love! Your love has scandalized me sweetly.
Boy	:	I swear to God.
Girl	:	I swear to God.
Kalapahada	:	You will stay with me forever from this day!
Gulnaz	:	We are not married. How can I stay with you?
Kalapahada	:	I agree to marry you, but what does your father think about our love?
Gulnaz	:	My father never disrespects my choice!
Kalapahada	:	Now you can tell your father about our love. Let him do the arrangement for our marriage.

[At this time, Suleiman Karrani has reached there.]

Suleiman	:	Kalapahada! Have you confessed your love to marry my daughter?

[Kalapahada and Gulnaz go apart and stand looking downward.]

Suleiman	:	Having heard this, I am very happy. I also

		agree to your proposal. But before that, I have a condition for you.
Kalapahada	:	What's that condition?
Suleiman	:	I am an Afghan, and you are a Hindu- so, if you want to marry my daughter, you must accept the Muslim religion.
Kalapahada	:	I can't give up my religion!
Suleiman	:	Then, you forget Gulnaz. She will never marry you.
Gulnaz	:	What do you say, *Abbajan*?
Suleiman	:	What I say is correct. If he doesn't give up his religion for the sake of love, how can I believe him? After the marriage, I thought I would make Kalapahada the General of my army. But for his religion, he is ready to throw away everything. A Hindu and an Afghan can't stay together as husband and wife. Both of them should accept one religion.
Kalapahada	:	If Gulnaz accepts the Hindu religion after the marriage, do you have any objection?
Suleiman	:	Impossible! Your Hindu religion won't accept my daughter.
Kalapahada	:	But for marriage, I can't readily accept your proposal to change my religion.
Suleiman	:	Then Kalapahada, you remember; all the doors of my heart are closed for you from today onwards. You have ruined my daughter's life. I will kill you.
Kalapahada	:	Will you kill me?
Suleiman	:	I will wipe your name from this world forever. You are a traitor. There is no place for the traitors to live in this world.

Kalapahada	:	A guest should be treated equally. It's against the religion.
Suleiman	:	If a guest goes beyond his limits, he is not a guest but an enemy. Then the punishment for him is 'death'.
Kalapahada	:	I am not a traitor. I accept that I love Gulnaz.
Gulnaz	:	If you love me truly, why don't you agree to this proposal?
Kalapahada	:	Well, I agree to your proposal.
Suleiman	:	Kalapahada, I am very much pleased with you. You are truly human. You are not my son-in-law. You are the General of my state- you are not a Hindu- you are an Afghan! You are not Kalapahada. Your name is Muhammad Farmuli since this day!

[Light off]

SCENE-VI

[In the room designed for evil plans, of Kalinga's Palace, Rudranarayan and Mukunda Deva are engaged in plotting the conspiracy.]

Mukunda Deva: I sent Kalapahada to Suleiman's palace with a 'Peace Proposal'. But I can't believe he will be the General of Suleiman's army, giving up his religion. Kalapahada is a traitor.

Rudranarayan : Today, from the entire 'Land of Banga', a voice is raised against him. A Hindu can give up his religion for a Muslim daughter! Now the people hate me for this. This Kalapahada came to me one day, hoping to get a job. I appointed him a soldier in my army. I promoted him to the General of my army post, having been pleased with his skill and efficiency. But now you see the consequence of that.

Mukunda Deva: My dear Rudranarayan! After being defeated by us in the battle, Suleiman Karrani tried his best to split our power. After Kalapahada reached him with the

	'Treaty Proposal', he kept Kalapahada under his control with a conspiracy. The means of this conspiracy is Suleiman's daughter.
Rudranarayan :	You may be right- why was Kalapahada trapped in the conspiracy?
Mukunda Deva:	In politics, many incidents happen. You please forget all this. Now Kalapahada is our enemy – we should be alert and aware of him.
Rudranarayan :	I don't have any fear.
Mukunda Deva:	Yes. I make you aware that, as you don't surrender to Akbar, so there is danger from the side of the Mughals. Suleiman of the 'Land of Gouda' is also your enemy. Then, it is your responsibility to protect your land.

[Ramachandra Bhanja comes- He is the taxpayer King to Mukunda Deva.]

Ramachandra :	When we lose faith in our people, others betray us!
Mukunda Deva:	Ramachandra Bhanja, what do you want to say?
Ramachandra :	What was the need to assign the responsibility of the combined army of Kalinga and Bhurishrestha to Kalapahada? Was there not an eligible Commander in Kalinga for that? After the victory, you also handed over the responsibility of Saptagram to Kalapahada!
Mukunda Deva:	You want to say here that it was our

	wrong decision to assign responsibility to Kalapahada while fighting with the Nawab of Gouda. We had many warriors in our regiment for the replacement of Kalapahada.
Ramachandra :	Why had they been deprived of?
Rudranarayan :	You don't have the right to ask me this question!
Ramachandra :	Neither of you is the son of this land. How will you develop your love for Kalinga, Telenga Mukunda Deva? Though you consider yourself the 'Gajapati' of Odisha, you are always dependent upon the people of the other states. So, the warriors of Kalinga will never help you at any time.
Mukunda Deva:	Shut up, Ramachandra!
Ramachandra :	What will you get if you forcibly stop my mouth? The Kalapahada you have created today will be detrimental to Kalinga in the future. We are waiting for that.

[Ramachandra leaves.]

Rudranarayan :	How can a taxpayer, King Ramachandra Bhanja, respond to the Gajapati?
Mukunda Ceva:	He is also a traitor. I will punish him shortly. He will be sentenced to death.

[Light off]

SCENE-VII

[Kalapahada sits solemnly. Gulnaz comes to him.]

Gulnaz	:	Why are you looking so indifferent today?
Kalapahada	:	The apprehensions I had with earlier have become true now. I have become a Muslim, giving up the Hindu religion. It has been spread all over the 'Land of Banga'. All the people now hate me. They insult me everywhere, saying me the sinful and the unholy.
Gulnaz	:	You went to your village. What did happen there?
Kalapahada	:	All the villagers segregated my mother. She left for Brindavan unhappily.
Gulnaz	:	You couldn't meet her.
Kalapahada	:	No- I could neither meet her nor talk to her. Gulnaz, I can't live bearing so much insult- I will go mad.
Gulnaz	:	All these are because of me. Had you not married me, you would not have suffered much.
Kalapahada	:	No, Gulnaz, I loved you. It's not your fault. Neither can I leave you today, nor

		can I give up my religion.
Gulnaz	:	What do you think of now?
Kalapahada	:	I will return and embrace my religion!
Gulnaz	:	How will you return?
Kalapahada	:	All the people of our village told me to consult the Pundits residing in *Srikshetra*. If they want, I can return to my Hindu religion. But Gulnaz, if I return to the Hindu religion, will you change your religion?
Gulnaz	:	You are my husband, my God. Your religion is my religion. Why do you ask me this?

[Suleiman Karrani comes in.]

Suleiman	:	Kalapahada! Your Hindu religion won't accept you so easily.
Kalapahada	:	I will try my best, *Abbajan*! I am sure that the Pundits in *Srikshetra* will forgive me and consecrate me to the Hindu religion.
Suleiman	:	Who do you have faith in? Do you believe the orthodox Hindu Pundits?
Kalapahada	:	No. I have faith in Lord Jagannatha. I have heard it from my mother. He is *Patitapabana* (Of the distressed and of the sinful). He is the God of the devotees. If He wants, the impossible can also be made possible.
Suleiman	:	My best wishes are always with you. If your religion doesn't accept you, Suleiman Karrani's doors are always open for you.

Kalapahada : *Abbajan*!
Suleiman : If you are depressed and disappointed at any time, you come to me. I will wait for you, my son, till the moon and the sun are in the sky.

[Light off]

SCENE-VIII

[Wearing a typical dhoti and a baniyan, Kalapahada stands calmly with folded hands- Three Brahmans are standing before him.]

Brahmana-I : Is your name Kalachanda? By birth, are you a Brahman? You are from the 'Land of Banga'.

Brahman-II : Your name has been changed to Kalapahada after marrying a Muslim girl!

Kalapahada : Yes, the great priest. It was a big mistake in my life. I am worried about that. Now I want to return to my earlier religion. I am not Kalapahada, but the Hindu Brahman Rajivlochan Ray.

Brahman-III : What are you now?

Kalapahada : I am the General of the Army of Nawab Suleiman Karrani!

Brahman-III : What will you do, if you leave your wife, children, and the Army's General post?

Kalapahada : I have never thought of what I will do next. Giving up my religion, I suffer significantly from the woes of religion. I don't need anything more. I want to lead my life as was earlier.

Brahman-I	: You went to *Gajapati*. He made you return. Having recited an Islamic oath of allegiance, you have married. You eat beef. You have made unholy your body. After that, you are telling to return to your religion. Once the body is made sinful, how can it be made holy?
Kalapahada	: Is there no way prescribed in your scriptures?
Brahman-I	: Had there been any means, we would have told you! This body is an earthen pot. Once broken, it turns into pieces. Can it be an earthen pot again if we try hard to unite all the parts? Giving up religion is easy, but once anybody has accepted a different religion, he cannot return to his earlier religion.
Kalapahada	: You are the Pundits. If you want, you can find the way!
Brahman-II	: We are indeed Pundits, but we have not written the religious texts. God has written all this. So, how can we modify His writings?
Kalapahada	: Please be compassionate to me, Brahmans. Bless me and help me return to my religion.
Brahman-I	: Don't share your sins. We can't do anything more.
Kalapahada	: Then, shall I return?
Brahman-II	: It will be right for you to return! Let's move, all my Pundits!

[All the Pundits are about to leave.]

Kalapahada	:	Please listen to me! (Taking a return, the Pundits look at him.) Of the religion's rigidity and God's pride, you compel me to return from this place- that's your wrong decision- you are committing a crime!
Brahman-I	:	Shut up, the sinner. Hold your tongue!
Brahman-II	:	The Hindu religion is not a cow shed where; at any time, one can leave it and return to join here whimsically. It is the Vedic Sanatan Religion. It was established a thousand years ago. Nobody dares to make it unholy.
Kalapahada	:	I will defame it!
Brahman-I	:	Neither you nor your fourteen generations of your family can do? If I give you a blow, you will fall.
Kalapahada	:	Hold on! (Kalapahada raises his sword. Brahmans, stop there.) I had promised not to brandish the sword. I will perform *yajya* (sacrifice), holding *pothi* (religious books) and *kamandal* (oblong water pot)! But today, you have forced me to wave the sword again. You have made me ferocious. Hey, Pundits! I swear, I will ruin your pride and arrogance one day. I will uproot your religion and throw it into the Bay of Bengal. You won't be able to see a temple of the Hindu God or Goddess. I will destroy everything- I will devastate all!

[The Brahmans react and Kalapahada leaves the spot.]
[Light off]

SCENE-IX

[Suleiman Karrani walks disturbed in Gouda Darwar. Kalapahada reaches there. He is with a dhoti and a baniyan and returns from Kalinga.]

Suleiman : It was known that the Hindu religion won't accept you so quickly! (Suleiman laughs.) I guess, you have returned disappointed from Kalinga!
Kalapahada : Yes!
Suleiman : I knew, "Once an individual gives up a religion, it's impossible for him to return to that religion." When you placed before me the marriage proposal for my daughter, I denied Gulnaz's acceptance of the Hindu religion. I compelled you to accept Islam religion. Now you can understand why I told you all this!
Kalapahada : I can understand now. The way I was insulted in Kalinga hurts me a lot. I will take revenge on them one by one. I swear, 'Not a single temple will exist in Utkal.' The water of Mahanadi will be bloodstained!

Suleiman	:	I have waited for that. I can understand how you have been humiliated. Your insult is my insult. I want that what you want. We have to invade Kalinga.
Kalapahada	:	Please, you assign me the responsibility. I will return from there once I devastate Kalinga entirely.
Suleiman	:	We can't succeed anything in anger. We have to chalk out our plans meticulously. We have to invade Kalinga strategically. I have already planned. We will invade Kalinga simultaneously with two military forces.
Kalapahada	:	With two military forces?
Suleiman	:	Yes, I will lead one military force. My son Baijid will lead another in which you will be the General. If we invade Kalinga from two directions, the King of Kalinga can't defend.

[Ramachandra comes in.]

Ramachandra	:	I will lead the third regiment to fight against Mukunda Deva.
Suleiman	:	Come, Ramachandra- you are welcome to the Gouda Darwar. Kalapahada, he is Ramachandra Bhanja, the King of Saranga Gada.
Kalapahada	:	That I know!
Ramachandra	:	I am not the King of Saranga Gada (a piece of state land). I am the owner of the 'Throne of Kalinga'. I don't accept the Telenga Mukunda Deva as the Gajapati of Kalinga.

Kalapahada	:	That will be decided after the Battle of Kalinga is over. Please be prepared for the battle. Could you leave me alone for a while?
Suleiman	:	Ramachandra, please come with me. We will discuss.

[Both Ramachandra and Suleiman leave the place. Kalapahada gets infuriated, while recollecting the words of Brahman Pundits.]

Kalapahada	:	I will completely ruin the Jagannatha Temple.
		[Gulnaz comes in.]
Gulnaz	:	Before that, you should not be ruined!
Kalapahada	:	What do you say, Gulnaz?
Gulnaz	:	If Jagannatha and Allah are one, nobody is born on the Earth to ruin God.
Kalapahada	:	They have left me insulted!
Gulnaz	:	You will take revenge on Kalinga for a handful of people- this is wrong.
Kalapahada	:	Then, will I be a Muslim for my entire life?
Gulnaz	:	If you battle, can you return to your religion?
Kalinga	:	I will take revenge on Kalinga- Nobody can obstruct me from that!
Gulnaz	:	Well, this is right! You can fight with the King of Kalinga - but you swear to me – you will never ruin the temples of the Hindus. They have not harmed you at all.
Kalapahada	:	I can't promise you. Please don't force me.
		[Kalapahada leaves.]

Gulnaz : You are mistaken, Kalapahada – you are wrong!

[Light off]

SCENE-X

[Mukunda Deva and Durga Bhanja stand in the battle field.]

Mukunda Deva	:	General, I am perhaps the last King of Kalinga, after whose death the Afghan Rulers will govern Kalinga.
Durga Bhanja	:	Why do you say so, Maharaj?
Mukunda Deva	:	Our energy and ability get trapped and devastated in plotting the conspiracy. Our taxpayer, King Ramachandra Bhanja, via Shikhi-Manai, has betrayed us. The Goudas Nawab Suleiman Karrani invades Kalinga with two regiments.
Durga Bhanja	:	But why are those who have given the words to assist us silent now?
Mukunda Deva	:	I also thought of that. My friend, the King of Bhurishrestha also sits silently. Promising to help us, he is busy supporting the Mughal Emperor to conquer Chitor. Thus, to get help from others is futile.

	Anyway, we have to fight this battle.
Durga Bhanja	: Can the Kalinga Regiment obstruct many soldiers at a time?
Mukunda Deva	: I have decided to punish the agitators. Only obstructing and opposing Suleiman Karrani and Kalapahada's regiments is possible, once we neutralize the conspirators, the taxpayer Kings of the Kalinga Regiment.
Durga Bhanja	: Maharaj! Kalapahada and his regiment will reach Cuttack via Mayurbhanja and Chotnagpur jungle. Within a few days, Suleiman and his army will arrive at Jajpur. Who do you think to fight at this time?
Mukunda Deva	: Ramachandra Bhanja-
Durga Bhanja	: Will it be the right decision?
Mukunda Deva	: Before Kalapahada reaches Cuttack; I want to see Ramachandra Bhanja's demise. I have planned that Purandar Jagadeva will safeguard Sri Mandir with ten thousand soldiers. You will protect Barabati Fort with another ten thousand soldiers. Tell Parichha Divyasingh Pattanayak to take away Jagannatha from Sri Mandir. I will confront that traitor in the Battle at Tikiri, Gohara.

Durga Bhanja	:	Well, Maharaja. I am doing all the preparations for you.

[Durga Bhanja leaves.]

Mukunda Deva: Mahaprabhu Jagannatha! Now, it's your responsibility to save Kalinga.

[Ramachandra Bhanja comes.]

Ramachandra Bhanja	:	Will you save Kalinga? The King Telenga Mukunda Deva of the Chalukya dynasty!
Mukunda Deva	:	The traitor Ramachandra Bhanja! Being my taxpayer King and in alliance with the Afghans, you have invited Kalapahada to invade Kalinga!
Ramachandra Bhanja	:	You are the traitor, Mukunda Harichandan. How are you, Mukunda Deva? Having entered the Barabati Fort with your brothers in disguise, and killed Gajapati Narasingh Jena, you had celebrated the coronation of his brother Raghuram Jena for Kalinga's throne. Janarddhan Bidyadhar and I had known your trick. So, to fulfill your greed, you had imprisoned Janarddhan Bidyadhar and became the Gajapati of Kalinga after killing Raghuram Jena.
Mukunda Deva	:	Shut up, Ramachandra.

Ramachandra Bhanja	:	It's high time now; you should know about your betrayal and conspiracy. Soldiers, you attack now.
Mukunda Deva	:	The brave *paikas* (a particular caste of people engaged in the battlefield) of Odisha, who plotted a conspiracy against their own King, are ungrateful. They should be punished right now. Assault them.

[A decisive face-off is marked between Ramachandra Bhanja and Mukunda Deva. Mukunda Deva dies in the battle. Ramachandra Bhanja laughs loudly.]

Mukunda Deva	:	Jay Jagannatha (He falls down.)!
Ramachandra Bhanja	:	Now I am the Gajapati of Kalinga. *Veera Sri Gajapati Goudeswar Navakoti Karnnat Kalebargeswar* Ramachandra Bhanja.

[At this time, Kalapahada comes with his regiment.]

Ramachandra Bhanja	:	Come, Kalapahada. Mukunda Deva is killed on the battlefield. As per our conditions, I will be the Gajapati of Kalinga. There is no need for you to fight now. Return to your 'Land of Banga' with your troop.
Kalapahada	:	One not faithful to his King can't be believed in. No conspirator can sit on Kalinga's throne.

[Kalapahada comes forward to assault Ramachandra Bhanja. He gets surprised.]

Ramachandra Bhanja	:	What's this, Kalapahada? Will you fight with me?
Kalapahada	:	Suleiman Karrani will be crowned for Kalinga, but not you.
Ramachandra	:	You are a traitor.

[Ramachandra Bhanja comes forward waving the sword. Kalapahada attacks him with the sword. Ramachandra Bhanja falls there.]

[Light off]

SCENE-XI

[Rani Padmavati and Rajguru talk to each other.]

Rajguru : Have you received any information about the battle?

Padmavati : Yes, Gajapati died in the fight. A traitor set the last sun of Kalinga. We need help tracing Divyasingh Pattanayak. He hides somewhere, dislodging Jagannath from Sri Mandir.

Rajguru : But that traitor couldn't be Kalinga's Gajapati. Like a jackal, he died before Kalapahada.

Padmavati : Despite all this, Kalinga is not free now. The Afghan rulers will rule it. Is this your last wish, Jagannatha? For your safety, out of fear for the invaders, you hide yourself in an unknown place. Those invaders will proceed towards Sri Mandir and succeed 'Kalinga Throne'.

Rajguru : We are yet to determine Kalinga's fate, Maharani!

Padmavati : Jagannatha couldn't save the prestige of 'Maharani'. I have lost my land and I

have lost my husband. Now I am not the great Empress, but an ordinary widow.
[At this time, a soldier brings Mukunda Deva's crown and sword on a plate. Having seen those, Padmavati cries.]

Soldier : Gajapati's crown and sword-
Padmavati : The day Gajapati dies, the prince gets coronated. Today, Gajapati is no more- we also have no prince. I am left alone to see Kalinga's demise and downfall. What do you do, Jagannatha- you could not protect this land. You are the King of Kalinga, and Gajapati is your servant. Being a King, have you handed over the land to an Afghan? Why? Why did you do it?

[Kalapahada enters the fort at this time.]

Kalapahada : From this day onwards, the Afghans will rule the Barabati Fort.
Padmavati : (clearing the tearful eyes) You are then Kalapahada.
Kalapahada : Can I know who you are?
Padmavati : I am the Queen who lost his husband, King Mukunda Deva, the Queen of Padmavati.
Kalapahada : I say 'pranam' to you!
Padmavati : I don't receive any salute from a resentful Hindu cannibal.
Kalapahada : Yes, I am a resentful Hindu. I have promised to torture the Hindus. I will ruin all the Hindu temples! I will take revenge on the religion for which I have

Rajguru	:	been insulted and expelled from Kalinga. Do you think that the vast Hindu religion will be lost if you dismantle some of the Hindu temples? You have mistaken- stop assaulting the Hindus!
Kalapahada	:	You have forced me to invade and oppress others. I was a Hindu. My God was not Allah. I liked Jagannatha from my heart and soul. For Mukunda Deva, I fought against Suleiman Karrani. I made a mistake when I married a Muslim girl. For that, I requested Mukunda Deva to accept me again into Hindu religion and said to please forgive me- but he denied me. Your Brahman Pundits rejected my request. Why was I shown the path to return?
Padmavati	:	For that, have you come to take revenge on the entire Hindu race? Have you come to ruin the Jagannatha Temple?
Kalapahada	:	If Jagannatha wanted, it could be solved. But I struggle to live. If He is not mine, He can't be of anybody else. I will ruin Him completely.
Rajaguru	:	He is the one who wears rosary of worlds at His hair pore! He is the One who protects the fourteen worlds- how you can destroy Him, Kalapahada!
Kalapahada	:	You all wait to see what is going on in the coming days. The Afghans have already succeeded in ruling this Barabati Fort. Can you give me what you have stored in your store room, or will my soldiers plunder forcibly?

Padmavati : Until I am here at this fort- I am Maharani (Great Queen). To plunder before me is a crime!

[Padmavati hints with a clap. A maidservant comes with a plate full of gold, diamonds, and precious treasures and gives the same to Padmavati. While Padmavati hands over the same to Kalapahada, it is heard from the backdrop-]

"Kalapahada broke in and dismantled the iron fences,
And drank Mahanadi's water;
On a golden plate, offered diamonds
Mukunda Deva's Empress!"

Kalapahada : Now, you all leave the fort.

[The Empress Padmavati and Rajguru leave the spot- Kalapahada laughs violently.]

[Light off]

SCENE-XII

[Near the mouth of Chilika Lake, Jagannatha, Balabhadra, Subhadra and Sudarshana are kept on a bullock cart. A boat is tied on the bank of Chilika. Two servitors are discussing.]

Servitor-I	:	Hey Nana, are you aware of the state of affairs?
Servitor-II	:	What state of affairs are you talking of?
Servitor-I	:	What? Throughout the state, the message is spread that the Afghan General Kalapahada has invaded Kalinga, but you are unaware of that!
Servitor-II	:	Is Kalapahada Mughal or Afghan?
Servitor-I	:	Afghan. But both are of the same religion. Anyway, leave that. That bastard has devastated all our temples. Some villages are set on fire. Who knows what's in our destiny?
Servitor-II	:	Hey, what temples has he destroyed?
Servitor-I	:	Don't you know anything? He has destroyed Konark Temple, Ramachandi Temple, and Chaushathi Jogini Temple. Now, he keeps an eye on Jagannatha Temple.

Servitor-II	:	He is destroying many temples. Can't the deities do any harm to him? We worship Him. How can He protect us?
Servitor-I	:	You are talking nonsense. Can the deities go to fight against Kalapahada?
Servitor-II	:	What's the need for any battle? God can blow him away like cotton.

[Then Servitor-III comes with Divyasingh Pattanayak.]

Servitor-I	:	His Majesty! Have you traced any secret place where we can hide Lord Jagannatha?
Servitor-III	:	You are talking about a place to hide, but Jagannatha has turned into stone. Otherwise, why could He rest on the bullock cart on the bank of Chilika Lake? Neither could he protect Himself, nor could He save Gajapati!
Servitor-I	:	What do you say, Nana? What has happened to Gajapati?
Divyasingh	:	Gajapati breathed his last in the battle and left for heaven.

[Both the servitors cry.]

Servitor I & II	:	(in unison) No, sir. Please, don't say so.
Divyasingh	:	Jagannatha has put me on the horns of a dilemma. I am unable to decide what to do next. Gajapati died at the hands of the traitor Ramachandra Bhanja. I approached Chilika Lake by dislodging Jagannatha from Sri Mandir to a bullock cart. Kalapahada searches for Him inside the temple. But I am unable to trace a place where I can hide Him.
Servitor-I	:	His Majesty, I know one place. That is

Chhapalli. None of Kalapahada's family members can reach there. But we must cross this Chilika Lake on a boat.

Servitor-II : Yes, Bhaginna is right. There is no better place than Chhapalli.

Divya Singh : Well, immediately let Mahaprabhu be seated on the boat. By the time Kalapahada is informed, we must have crossed the mouth of this Chilika Lake.

[The Servitors have helped the three idols sit on the boat.]

Divyasingh : O Mahabahu! You are the priest of that baffled traveller! You are the steersman of the endless sea. You are the charioteer of life. If human life is empty and void, you are an heir to that void. If humans are alive, you are safe.

[The Servitors on the boat shout now.]

Servitor-III : His Majesty! The boat is ready now. Please come.

[Divyasingh sits on the boat. The boat moves ahead on waves of Chilika Lake.]

[Light off]

SCENE-XIII

[Kalapahada is infuriated now. He asks his spies.]

Kalapahada	:	Where is Jagannatha? Why can't you inform me about that?
Spy	:	We searched for Him everywhere, General, but we couldn't trace His whereabouts.
Kalapahada	:	Then, has He disappeared into the void? Someone else must have hidden Him somewhere!
Spy	:	We have asked all the servitors. We have killed some of them- we have set ablaze their houses-but nobody responds to us where Jagannatha resides now.
Kalapahada	:	Oh, you are all making me mad- anyway, I need Jagannatha!
Spy	:	Someone waits for you outside, General!
Kalapahada	:	Who's he?
Spy	:	He says that he is Dana Patra, the headman of Kokalagada!
Kalapahada	:	Why has he come here?
Spy	:	He doesn't tell us, but he may tell you!
Kalapahada	:	I don't have time to spare with an ordinary person.

Spy	: Lest we should get information. Please ask him.
Kalapahada	: Well. Send him inside!

[The spy leaves. Kalapahada says himself.]

Kalapahada	: Dana Patra; why has he come?
Dana Patra	: I salute to the General!
Kalapahada	: What happens?
Dana Patra	: Do you have any information about Lord Jagannatha?
Kalapahada	: Why do you ask me this?
Dana Patra	: Because I know the place where Lord Jagannatha is now!
Kalapahada	: How can I believe that you know?
Dana Patra	: It depends on you whether you believe or not. But I will help you reach Lord Jagannatha!
Kalapahada	: What will be your benefit?
Dana Patra	: I have come here to ask you that question- If I lead you to the place where Jagannatha is, how will you help me?
Kalapahada	: What do you want?
Dana Patra	: The grant of the estate Chabiskuda and Rahanga!
Kalapahada	: You will get that. I will also honour you with the title of Pahanta Singh!
Dana Patra	: How can I believe this?
Kalapahada	: Why do you doubt me?
Dana Patra	: Before you invaded Kalinga, Durga Bhanja and Ramachandra helped you, but you killed them. With what faith will I help you reach Lord Jagannatha?
Kalapahada	: I would like to thank the Emperor of Kalinga, Mukunda Deva, for nurturing so

	many traitors in the kingdom. Well, Dana Patra, if I kill you now?
Danapatra	: Then, you will never trace the whereabouts of Lord Jagannatha throughout your life.
Kalapahada	: You are clever and wise. Well, I will sign with you an agreement paper. Will you help me reach out to Jagannatha?
Dana Patra	: Be ready at the early dawn today- I will help you reach the right place!
	[Kalapahada laughs loudly.]

[Light off]

SCENE-XIV

[It's a jungle of Chhapalli. Lord Jagannatha, Balabhadra, Subhadra and Sudarshana are on a mound of Earth. The servitors stand near the sight. Some liquid clay drops are found on the bodies of the three idols. The servitors remove the same with the towels.]

Servitor-I : Is it the fate of Odisha, Mahaprabhu? We are not sure of our homes and villages. The soldiers of Kalapahada kill the public one by one.

Servitor-II : We, the humans are so insignificant. Were you destined to suffer? We still determine how long you will stay in this wild forest, leaving Ratnavedi.

Servitor-III : Having crossed such a long distance on the boat, you must have been tired- I am pressing your body gently.

[All three servitors gently press the limbs of the deities while washing them with towels. Divya Singh comes out at this moment.]

Divyasingh : If we were at the temple, we could have completed the mid-day waving of light before Lord Jagannatha. What have you

	arranged for 'food offering' (blessed food)?
Servitor-I	: I searched, but I didn't find anything. I brought some bowls of rice for me. I have cooked some out of that. We will offer it to Jagannatha. The day when we run out of the rice, like Jagannatha, we will also fast.
Divyasingh	: *Mahaprabhu*, who do you test, the devotee or yourself? You are omnipotent. The whole world is within you. Like the rosaries, you wear the stars and the planets on your neck. Why are you silent these days?
Servitor-II	: His Majesty! He is always the dumbfounded Vishnu. I have never seen a deity so tolerant in the world. He embraces the person who scolds Him out of anger and also the person who invokes Him in full devotion.
Divyasingh	: Well, complete your offerings to the deities. I have come here to pass you a message. Having entered Barabati Fort, Kalapahada has occupied the fort. The Empress and the councillors of the Royal Court have left that place. I don't know where they are now. I have to go to them. You will look after Jagannatha in my absence.
Servitor-III	: All of us are in bad days of Odisha. Let Mahaprabhu (Lord Jagannatha) save you under the shade of His Sudarshana Chakra.

[Saying pranam to Lord Jagannatha, Divyasingh leaves the place.]

Servitor-I : Hey Nana! Complete the celebration of offering. There is no torchlight for the night. We will be in darkness.

[At this time, Kalapahada, his soldiers, and Dana Patra reach there.]

Danapatra : Please see, General, Jagannatha is here.

Kalapahada : Oh! Here is Jagannatha, the Emperor of Kalinga!

Servitor-II : His Majesty! That is the wooden idol; how is He harmful to you? Why have you come here?

Kalapahada : I have come here to ruin your Lord Jagannatha forever! For this Jagannatha, Odisha's pride and prestige has touched the sky- I will set Him to fire and destroy completely. Soldiers, lodge Jagannatha on elephant's back up to Ganga River.

[Two elephants are brought. The servitors obstruct the soldiers while lodging Jagannatha on the elephant's back. The soldiers thrash them, and they are crawling in dust out of pain and subsequently lying flat on the ground. While singing, Bishar Mohanty comes beating a tabor hung on his neck. The elephants have come to the boat by the time the song ends. Four idols are on them. The servitors lament, lying flat on the ground. Taking Jagannatha, Kalapahada leaves the place along with his soldiers.]

Song : The sky falls, the Earth tears apart,
The sea laments, beating her head.
Four clouds of thunder getting perplexed,
The significant deluge advances.

Devotees request humbly with their palms
    folded,
Don't take that; that's our ruby basket.
If we don't see Him, We will lose our eyes.
That's our Jagannatha;
Without Him, the whole world is empty.

[Light off]

SCENE-XV

[Inside the Khorda Fort are Ramachandra Deva, Queen Shreeya Devi and Rajguru.]

Ramachandra : All betrayed my father for the throne. Taking advantage, Gouda Nawab Suleiman Karrani invaded Kalinga. The Barabati Fort, Cuttack, where the Gajapatis stayed to rule over Kalinga, is now under the surveillance of Suleiman Karrani's son Baijid. He is now the new ruler.

Shreeya Devi : Kalinga has no freedom, because of the traitor Ramachandra Bhanja, Kuni Samantara, and Shikhi Manai! The Afghans started ruling Kalinga. The Muslim rulers, Afghans, will rule over Kalinga. Was it Lord Jagannatha's wish?

Rajguru : Jagannatha also lost His pride. At midnight, Dana Patra of Kokalagada crossed the mouth of Chilika Lake with Kalapahada and reached there! The deity of this Odia race! An atheist like Kalapahada takes the adorable God of this race, loading on the back of an elephant up to the bank of

		River Ganga for burning- can any Odia bear to listen to this story?
Shreeya Devi	:	No, Kalapahada, if you try hard to set fire to Jagannatha, you can't burn Him.
Ramachandra	:	How do you say so?
Shreeya Devi	:	The Crown Prince! I know that Jagannatha is the imperishable Brahma. Brahma can neither be cut into pieces nor be burnt on fire. Nothing in the world can destroy it. Wherefrom is created all the five elements like Earth, air, water, fire and ether. Kalapahada is very insignificant before Him.
Rajaguru	:	Well, will Jagannatha return to Ratnavedi again, Maharani?
Shreeya Devi	:	He will surely return. He will show the brilliance and lustre of a thousand suns from the great void; the world will be shocked to see. That's why, if Jagannatha is the soul of Utkal, the land of Utkal is His body. Leaving the body, the soul can't stay alone.
Ramachadra	:	For that, we must fight! We have to drive the Afghans away from Kalinga soil!
Rajguru	:	Akbar has sent his General Mansingh to Kalinga to solve this problem. Perhaps the Mughals will battle with the Afghans.
Ramachandra	:	But Rajguru, remember one point; if there is a close fight between the Mughals and the Afghans, the Barabati Fort will go to the hands of the Mughals. For that, I am constructing a unique fort in Khordha. The Kings of eighteen native states of Odisha

stand by us. If Mansingh considers the 'Throne of Khordha' as unique and we are allowed by him to claim our rights on Jagannatha Temple, we can make a treaty with him. Otherwise, we will continue our battle against the Mughals and the Afghans.

[Light off]

SCENE-XVI

[On the bank of River Ganga, the idols of Jagannatha, Balabhadra, Subhadra, and Sudarshana are brought on the elephants. Kalapahada, Gulnaz and the soldiers stand there. Running from a distance, Bishar Mohanty stands at a nearby place. Kalapahada instructs his soldiers.]

Kalapahada : This Jagannatha is the symbol of pride for Odisha! If Jagannatha is destroyed, the backbone of Odisha is broken. Gajapati Mukunda Deva, though tried a lot, could save neither him nor his Jagannatha. Today, I will ruin that Jagannatha forever. (Subsequently, he orders his soldiers.) You all take these four idols and throw them into the fire.

Gulnaz : No, no; Kalachand!

Kalapahada : Shut up-

[The soldiers bring Jagannatha from the elephant's back and cast into the fire ablaze. Bishar Mohanty shouts at a distance.]

Bishar : Hey, the sinner- one who is the King of the whole world- the Lord of emancipation of innumerable souls-the robust shelter of the diseased- you want to burn in fire-

Religion can't forgive you- you will be ruined naturally.

[A song is heard on the stage.]

Song : To whom the sun, moon, planets and stars invoke;
That's burning now and becomes a flame.
One, the steadfast faith of innumerable hearts,
That casts off his body and breathes His last.
Indeed, the mystery of the Almighty, how helpless He is;
Odia's courage is lost, and his heart is torn apart.
Say how the devotees can live without God;
That's my Jagannatha;
Without Him, the whole world is empty and meaningless.

[At the back of the stage, the fire burns fiercely. Suddenly, Kalapahada feels unbearable pain in his whole body.]

Kalapahada : Why does my body react abruptly? My body aches, as if it were burning in fire and cut into pieces-

[Gulnaz gets hold of him.]

Gulnaz : What happened to you?

Kalapahada : I can't bear so much pain, Gulnaz!

[Kalapahada rolls on the ground- Gulnaz says, shouting at the soldiers.]

Gulnaz : Stop burning the idols- Immerse them in River Ganga!

[When the soldiers immerse the half-burnt idols in the Ganga, from a distance, Bishar Mohanty runs, calling 'O, Jagannatha' and jumps into the water.]

[Light off]

SCENE-XVII

[It's Umrao's home. In front of the building are four half-burnt logs on a bullock cart. Umrao comes out of his house with an axe. Then Bishar Mohanty reaches there, having a tabor on his neck.]

Bishar	:	Can you hear me, brother?
Umrao	:	What happened?
Bishar	:	Is this your home?
Umrao	:	Yes, who are you?
Bishar	:	I am a Vaishnab Brahman- I wander door to door for begging. I am from Odisha.
Umrao	:	How have you reached here, covering such a long distance? Have you come here for begging?
Bishar	:	I have been searching for my beloved God on the bank of Ganga for the last six months- I am unable to trace Him. I jumped into the Ganga but couldn't find Him. Is there anybody who knows where he has disappeared!
Umrao	:	Of whom are you talking?
Bishar	:	Kalapahada brought Jagannatha loading on the elephant to the bank of this Ganga River!

Umrao	: That story is six months old. I have also heard that.
Bishar	: What have you heard?
Umrao	: He is Gouda King's son-in-law. He set on fire the idol of Lord Jagannatha on the bank of the Ganga; then, his whole body broke apart and his wife threw the half-burnt idols into the Ganga River!
Bishar	: Where are all those idols?
Umrao	: Who knows where they are? They must have been washed away in the river!
Bishar	: Had they been floated, they would have reached ashore?
Umrao	: Have you searched for Him all around?
Bishar	: Since that day, I have been searching for Him on the bank of Ganga. I am unable to trace Him.
Umrao	: If you don't find Him, you can't. Well, what will you do, if you find?
Bishar	: He is the wooden idol of God. If I got a little piece of Him, I would worship. Who else can build such an idol? Well, brother! What do you do?
Umrao	: I do fishing in this Ganga. Nowadays, who knows what has happened? I am surprised not to see a fish on the river bank.
Bishar	: Do you return from the river daily without any catch?
Umrao	: What can I do? Some days earlier, I came across four half-burnt logs at the river bank. I brought these logs to my house for firewood. Today I can't fish . I am going to chop the wooden logs!

Bishar	:	Are the half-burnt logs four in number?
Umrao	:	Yes! I have loaded on this bullock cart. I have to unload them! (At this time, someone calls outside, 'O, Umrao'.) Saint, I am coming soon.

[After Umrao leaves, Bishar Mohanty runs to the bullock cart immediately. He scratches those half-burnt logs. He traces some pieces of silken clothes wrapped around them.]

Bishar	:	I have found! These silken clothes, these smearing- I am sure that, this is my adorable Lord Jagannatha. O, *Mahaprabhu*! I have heard the scriptures that nobody can destroy you. Neither can earth, air, water, fire, nor an invader's heinous mentality harm you. Your wooden bodies are wrapped with silken clothes- you are my Jagannatha. It's the proof, but how will I take you back from here?
Umrao	:	(Entering) A known person came here; I was talking to him- well, Saint, what will you do now?
Bishar	:	Nobody knows me here. Being baffled, I have been roaming in this 'Land of Banga' for the last six months- there is no certainty of my stay and food here. If you allowed me to stay at least for one or two days- after recovering myself, I would return to my state!
Umrao	:	Alright, He is a Vaishnava Saint. He requests me for help, how can I deny him? Please, be seated on the verandah.

I am chopping these logs, otherwise, how can we cook?

[Bishar Mohanty runs to get hold of Umrao.]

Bishar : No, these are uncommon heavenly logs! Will you cut these into pieces? I have seen the good firewood for cooking. Let's move together to bring them-
Umrao : What kind of wood are these?
Bishar : The wet wood will catch fire slowly- please come with me!

[Bishar Mohanty drags Umrao.]
[Light off]

SCENE-XVIII

[Here's a place well-girdled by the jungle in Khordha. The Fort of Khordha is observed from a distance. Ramachandra Deva stands firmly. Three servitors stand beside him.]

Servitor-I : His Majesty! The pride of Odisha shatters. We couldn't protect Lord Jagannatha.

Servitor-II : Dana Patra of Kokalagada reached there with Kalapahada. He was a traitor. He didn't look at Jagannatha for his greed for the grant of rent-free land. His family will ruin. Nobody will stay in his family to do any ritual for him!

Servitor-III : What could we have done before Kalapahada's vast regiment? He loaded Mahaprabhu on the elephant's back before us. We are torn apart, Maharaj!

Ramachandra : I have received all the information- for these traitors, the Kaling Throne gets bloodstained time and again. For these people today Lord Jagannatha … (Ramachandra stops for a while), well I can't say more!

Servitor-I : His Majesty! What has happened to Lord Jagannatha? Please tell us.

Ramachandra	: Kalapahada has burnt Jagannatha's idol on the bank of Ganga!
All Servitors	: Hey Jagannatha! (Saying so, all the servitors cry.)
Servitor-I	: Can't Lord Jagannatha return to Sri Mandir, Puri?
Servitor-II	: Can't we see Lord Jagannatha anymore? O, Kalia, my Kaliasuna-
Servitor-III	: His Majesty, please, you do something. Who knows Odisha without Jagannatha?
Ramachandra	: What shall I do now? I also struggle for my identity. I am not the Gajapati of Utkal. After the Afghans occupied the Barabati Fort, Baijid became the Emperor of Kalinga. Now, as per the instructions of Akbar, the General Mansingh reached Odisha. He fought against Baijid. The Afghans were defeated in the battle. The Mughals ruled over Cuttack. I have been fighting against the Mughals and the Afghans to give a unique identity to the 'Throne of Khordha'- Jagannatha knows when the bad days will be over.
Servitor-I	: Jagannatha is not here. How will he know? His Majesty, Our blessings are always with you. For the battle you have continued, be a winner in that!
Servitor-II	: Is it true that Kalapahada had burnt Mahaprabhu in fire? Nay, my mind says; nobody can destroy Him- Nobody can destroy Him-

[Like a lunatic, he leaves that place- Others watch him.]
[Light off]

SCENE-XIX

[It's night. A pin drop silence pervades everywhere. Four logs are loaded on the bullock cart before Umrao's house. Bishar Mohanty comes to the cart with a tabor in his hands and says.]

Bishar : O, Jagannatha, having faith in you, the Odia race lives- if you disappear, Odisha will be empty. Though Kalapahada has burnt your idols, I know your Brahma still resides within the half-burnt idols- I searched for you at many places, but I couldn't trace you anywhere- show me the path, Jagannatha- if I find Brahmas, Kalinga's Gajapati will install you again by changing your bodies! (Nabakalebara) *[A song is played on the stage.]*

Song : You are the soul of the devotees,
You are their life-source.
How can you severe that attachment with them?
That Brahma the three worlds have not seen ever,
Today, the devotee has seen that one.
As if the clouds showered devotional nectar,

> The thirst of the pied crested cuckoos gets satisfied,
> The poor are with God's plenty,
> The sky and the earth sing,
> And the air sings of the union of God and the devotee;
> This Maha Mantra, He is my Jagannatha;

Without Him, the whole world is empty and meaningless.
[By the time the song ends, Bishar Mohanty revolves around the logs; a log suddenly emerges while he pulls. Bishar becomes very happy.]

Bishar : Well, I have got. I have found the Brahma- but the entire world doesn't know what Brahma is made of. Thus, I won't see you, nor will I touch you. Let you be mysterious for me forever!

[Bishar Mohanty wraps one towel on his eyes, and one in his hand brings Brahmas from the four idols and keeps it inside the tabor- subsequently, he opens the towel from his eyes. Then, Umrao reaches there.]

Umrao : What are you doing here at the dead of the night?
Bishar : No, nothing.
Umrao : I don't have firewood at home. I have found some logs from the river bank of Ganga. When I try to chop these logs, you stop me.
Bishar : Well, you see, Umrao! You have allowed me to stay at your home, having faith in me; I am your friend. I will never tell you anything wrong- apart from that; I am also

		a Vaishnava saint. The Saint must think and do something for the betterment of the world- if you believe me- you listen to my words, what you call the 'log', that is the half-burnt body of Mahaprabhu, Jagannatha.
Umrao	:	It's false! Your Jagannatha's idol is one!
Bishar	:	Have you ever seen Jagannatha Temple at Puri?
Umrao	:	No-
Bishar	:	Have you ever seen the 'Rathayatra' or Chariot Festival?
Umrao	:	Where will I get money to visit for so long? I live in poverty-
Bishar	:	Then, you hear me, Jagannatha is not a single idol; there are four idols: Jagannatha, Balabhadra, Subhadra, and Sudarshana.
Umrao	:	They are stored on my homestead land- I am a sinner- Instead of worshipping, I think of using them as firewood! Had you not come here, I would have committed a great sin!
Bishar	:	Nay, Umrao, the burnt or broken idols are never worshipped- they are immersed.
Umrao	:	Then, what will I do now?
Bishar	:	As per the scriptures, the wooden idols will be buried under the ground- both of us will dig the ground and bury them here!
Umrao	:	Then the temple will be empty. Wherefrom will Jagannatha come?
Bishar	:	He will come, indeed. The way from one

lamp light, a thousand lamp lights are lit; similarly, from a part of the wooden idol, new idols can be born. I am taking small portions of those idols with me! If any Gajapati looks at them with reverence, Jagannatha will be mounted on bejewelled throne in Sri Mandir again.

Umrao : Are you speaking the Truth?

Bishar : I still wait for that day to come. If it comes, I swear to you; I will take you to visit the temple of Lord Jagannatha at Puri one day. Had you not been here, I would not have found Him.

Umrao : Who knows whether it's in my fate or not!

Bishar : Be assured that you will visit Puri- Umrao! We are late; let's move to bury the idols under the ground.

[Light off]

SCENE-XX

[Bishar Mohanty comes hanging a tabor on his neck- He is unable to walk properly. He has a fever, and his face is savvy with beard. Because of the evening, he rests at the step of a house. Then, an older woman comes out to wave the light before Goddess and sees Bishar.]

Old Woman	:	O Saint, who are you? Why are you sitting here on the step?
Bishar	:	I am a pilgrim, Maa. Taking a bath from Ganga, I was returning to my home. I am tired now. Having seen the night approaching, I am sitting here. I will go to rest on the temple's verandah. Tomorrow morning, I will resume my journey.
Old Woman	:	What do you say, Master? Where will you sleep at night? Come to my home!
Bishar	:	Nay, Maa! Why will I be a burden to you? I leave now!
Old Woman	:	Alright! The saints are like our guests. If you feel staying here is a sin, you can leave.
Bishar	:	What do you say, Maa? If I stay here, Will I earn a sin? No, because of me, you will

be in trouble. Well, perhaps God wants me to stay at your home- thus, where I will go- let's move.

[Bishar steps into her house- the older woman leads him- then, both come out to sit on the verandah.]

Bishar : Maa, sprinkle water over here- I will keep my tabor!

Old Woman : O Saint, you are in a Brahman's family. The surroundings are smeared with *gobar pani* (Water mixed with cow dung is considered sacred in Hindu way of life).

Bishar : Maa, my Guru had donated to me this tabor at the time of consecration. Thus, I worship it like a deity! My Guru taught me, "Brahma is only the Truth, and the whole world is false." What you see in this world is false. Brahma is one and only Truth. Brahma is everywhere, even in the worms, insects, earth, sky, etc. So, thinking of Brahma inside my tabor, I worship. Will it be right for me to put him on the ground?

Old Woman : Well, I sprinkle water over here!

Bishar : Yes, Maa; it's now evening. If you bring incense sticks and lamp, I will light the lamp and wave it.
[Old Woman gets shocked.]

Old Woman : Alright! (She leaves.)

Bishar : O, Jagannatha, as you wish?

[Older woman brings water and sprinkles over there. Bishar keeps his tabor there. She hands over incense sticks and lamp to

him- Bishar waves the light- then prostrates on the ground to surrender before the tabor.]

Old Woman : Do you worship this tabor every day?
Bishar : Man worships stone as God. So, this tabor is my God! While I wander on the road, I am not sure of my stay. So I don't get any chance to worship it. The day I stay at someone's house, I adore there. My home is at Kujung, Cuttack, Odisha. After I reach there, I will worship it every day.
Old Woman : O Saint! Your style of worship is so strange!
Bishar : Maa! Some people worship wood, while others worship trees. Similarly, I adore my tabor as God. Well, where are your other members of the family?
Old Woman : I had two sons and daughters-in-law. During Kalapahada's invasion, he entered my house and killed them all. I am the only one left!
Bishar : Like a comet, he was an evil planet. He appeared in Utkal's sky and ruined everything.
Old Woman : Wandering from village to village, he killed people, and at last, he entered Sri Mandir and annihilated the three idols. Can we be able to visit Jagannatha anymore?
Bishar : Maa! He is a fallen man. Jagannatha is *Darubrahma* (The *Brahma* encapsulated within the wood.) Can he destroy 'Brahma'? One day, you will see Brahma

	coming out of the ground and that will be mounted and worshipped in Sri Mandir.
Old Woman	: Who knows whether that chance will come to us?
Bishar	: You are so blessed that the Brahma itself is placed at your home. What can be better than this?
Old Woman	: Well, Saint, what do you want for dinner?
Bishar	: Don't worry about me, Maa! Having a glass of water, I can sleep.
Old woman	: What's this? At my home, you will sleep without food. I have cooked for me. I will serve you what I am with. You will have it. You have walked so long. Have you had anything earlier? Please be seated here- I am bringing that. (She leaves.)
Bishar	: O, Jagannatha, as you wish? (He says 'Pranam' to Lord Jagannatha.)

[*The Old Woman comes out of the kitchen with a plate decorated with Rice, Dal and leafy vegetables. Bishar Mohanty sits there. The older woman keeps the plate on the ground and puts a jug of water beside him.*]

Old woman	: O, Saint! I have served you what I had. Please have it!
Bishar	: Maa, what you have served me affectionately is better than *Mahaprasad*. But, without offering it to my God, I generally don't take food! Thus, I will have it after I offer *naibedya* to my God (the fruits or eatables offered to the deity).
Old woman	: I have served you rice, dal and leafy vegetables. Will your God receive this?

Bishar	: He is the God who understands our senses well. He is *Bhabagrahi*. He eats fragments of grains of rice while served affectionately.

[Bishar Mohanty worships the food with water- suddenly; the Old Woman senses the smell of Mahaprasad there.]

Old Woman	: Where does the smell of *Abhada* (Offerings made to Lord Jagannatha) come from? This smell comes from Sri Mandir only. Wherefrom does the scent of *Mahaprasad* come to my home?
Bishar	: Have I not told you that if you serve Him the fragments grains of rice with love and affection, He will receive the same happily? After worshipping this food with water, it gets converted to *Mahaprasad*. (Bishar gives the same to the Old Woman.) You receive this, *Prasad*. He puts the same in her mouth.

(A song is played on the stage.)

Song	: You won't see any God in the world, like Him; He receives food from devotees with affection. If served to Him in devotion, cooking a morsel of rice, The same food becomes *Abhada Mahaprasad*. Omnipresent God, He is everywhere; He is the savior of all; who can harm Him?

> If Kalapahada invades a thousand times,
> The *Singhadwar* of Sri Mandir will remain intact.
> Let the *Patitapaban* flag flutter forever,
> That's my Jagannatha.

Without Him, the whole world is empty and meaningless.

Old Woman : Yes, this is indeed the taste of *Abhada*. I can't believe this. Don't I dream, or is it real? Here are the smell of *Mahaprasad* and the taste of *Abhada*. After offering *Anna* (Rice) to Lord Jagannatha only, it becomes *Mahaprasad*. O, Saint! Is the God of your tabor Jagannatha?

Bishar : Jagannatha is everywhere. He is omnipresent; he resides in bodily forms. Because of Him, you feel the taste of *Mahaprasad*. Have I not told you that Kalapahada can't destroy Him? One day, He will be mounted in Sri Mandir- This is the Supreme Truth! It is right.

Old Woman : It seems to me, your words will be true! He is the absolute Truth! O, Jagannatha- I salute you a thousand times.

[Light off]

SCENE-XXI

[Ramachandra Deva, Shreeya Devi and Rajguru are talking inside the Khordha Fort.]

Ramachandra : I have received information from the spy that Baijid died in the fight between Mansingh and the King of Kalinga. The Afghans were defeated in the battle and left Kaling forever. Now, the Mughals will rule over Cuttack.

Shreeya Devi : How will we benefit, if the Mughals or the Afghans rule over Cuttack? The Muslims will govern the Kalinga state. Mansingh must have thought of controlling Khordha state.

Rajguru : Khordha state won't surrender before the Mughals so easily, Rajamata (the Queen Mother)! We will continue our battle as earlier.

[A messenger comes with information.]

Messenger : Let there be victory for *Yuvaraj* (The crown King)! Mansingh has sent a Mughal General for a visit to you.

Ramachandra : Let him come!

Messenger	:	As you wish!

[The Messenger leaves.]

Ramachandra : Why has Mansingh sent his Commander?

[The Mughal General comes in.]

Commander : Let there be victory for the King of Khordha!

Ramachandra : You are joking with me, the Mughal General! Neither am I the King of Khordha nor has it received any special status.

Commander : Your father had an excellent relationship with the Mughal Badsaha. That's why Mansingh declared Khordha a unique state. From this day onwards, you are the Gajapati of Khordha. You will have complete freedom for managing Sri Mandir!

Rajguru : Let there be victory for Gajapati Ramachandra Deva!

Ramachandra : This victory is not mine. It's Lord Jagannatha's victory. Please convey my 'best wishes' to the Mughal General, Mansingh. I am ever grateful to him for the decision he has taken.

Commander : I leave now, Gajapati. May God protect you! Goodbye!

Rajguru : I will arrange everything for the 'Coronation' ceremony, *Rajmata*!

Padmavati : Please, hold on! Slow down a bit! Nowadays, the *Ratnasighasana* (Bejewelled Throne) in Sri Mandir is empty. How can you arrange for the 'Coronation' ceremony in the state where Lord Jagannath is missing?

Rajguru	:	But Kalapahada has burnt Jagannatha's idol on the bank of Ganga. How can we find Jagannatha again?
Ramachandra	:	If anybody destroys Jagannatha's idol, is there any system prescribed in our scriptures to reinstall Lord Jagannatha at the *Ratnavedi*?
Rajguru	:	There is a system mentioned in the *Skandapuran* for the *Nabakalebara* of Lord Jagannatha. But we must take the Brahmas from the old idols and install them into the newer ones. Then, those will be regarded as the *Darubrahmas*!
Ramachandra	:	But where will we find the Brahmas?

[At this time, someone beats the tabor.]

Ramachandra : O, messenger! Who beats the tabor outside? Who beats this tabor near the Khordha Fort? (The Messenger comes.)
Messenger : A Vaishnava Saint who has come to meet you.
Ramachandra : You can allow him to step in.
Messenger : As you wish!

[The Messenger leaves and Bishar Mohanty enters beating the tabor.]

Ramachandra : Who are you? Why are you beating the tabor like this?
Bishar : It's the time for the Brahmas to descend. After a long gap, the four idols will be mounted on *Ratnasinghasana* (Bejewelled Throne). I am chanting the sacred name of God to welcome them.
Ramachandra : Will Brahmas get down? What do you

		say?
Bishar	:	Can *Ratnasinghasana* be empty forever? Jagannatha won't sit there?
Ramachandra	:	For that only, we celebrate *Nabakalebara*.
Rajguru	:	But if Brahmas are not installed in the newer wooden idols, those can't be called '*Darubrahma*'.
Shreeya Devi	:	I have heard the *Daruvigrahs* (wooden idols) were made during the rule of the King Jajati Keshari, with the help of Jagatguru Shankarcharya, after arranging an *Ashwamedha Yajna* (horse sacrifice). After Acharya Bharati collected the live *shalagrams* (a black stone worshipped as Vishnu and considered auspicious) from Nepal, the Brahmas were installed in the wooden idols. But the Brahmas were destroyed after Kalapahada had burnt them in fire. Then, how can we celebrate *Nabakalebara*?
Bishar	:	I have kept the Brahmas. His Majesty, Kalapahada threw the Brahmas into the Ganga as he couldn't burn them. At that moment, Umrao received the half-burnt idols and stored them at his home. I brought out all those Brahmas from the idols. I have installed them all at Gadakujang to worship.

[Ramachandra embraced Bishar Mohanty affectionately.]

Ramachandra : Bishar Mohanty, you are blessed. The people of Kalinga will remember your fame and glory till the moon and sun are in the sky. Rajguru, you can arrange the celebration of Nabakalebara, making the idols with the recitation of eighty-four prayers as per the directives of *Skandapuran*. Jagannatha Mahaprabhu will be mounted on *Ratnavedi* again. This day will be the great day of our happiness.

Shreeya Devi : Have patience, my son! We can't start Jagannatha's work without His wish. Kalinga is not independent. The independent King of Kalinga is no more. At this time, you are going to arrange the *Nabakalebara* ceremony. What I have heard is that first of all, people are on a *banajaga jatra* (night-awake journey), and then a *yajna* is arranged before *Darubruksha* (the tree selected for idols); subsequently, the chosen trees are cut down. Then, the bullock carts carry the cut-down trees to make the idols. From this day onwards, Nabakalebara of Lord Jagannatha will be celebrated every twelve years. Neither you nor I will be here in future. But it will be enshrined in the pages of history that Nabakalebara starts from here. Jay Jagannatha!

[The phrase 'Jay Jagannatha' is reverberated everywhere.]
[Light Off]

SCENE-XXII

[*It's the road. Some people stand, and there is a vast crowd. A servitor says.*]

Servitor-I : Hey, Scoundrel. Why have you joined the crowd? Side, please!
[*An older woman comes and asks.*]
Old Woman : Hello, my son! What's here? Why is here a huge crowd?
Servitor-I : You don't understand anything! Everywhere is heard the voice for the celebration of *Nabakalebara*. Do you know this or not? Well, side please- *Daru* loaded on to the bullock carts comes.
Old Woman : *Daru* comes!
Servitor-I : After Maa Mangala's order in the dream, the trees are selected for idols and worshipped; those trees are cut down and brought to the bullock carts. Jagannatha's idol will be made from that. The other three deities will also be made from them.
Old Woman : Is it true that Jagannatha's idol will be made? Four deities will be mounted on *Ratnavedi*! I can't believe this- Kalapahada

	set them on fire on the bank of the Ganga. Where did Jagannatha come from?
Servitor-I	: Hey, Kalapahada will burn! He is so insignificant- if I slap him, he will fall. He showed his terror and menace unnecessarily, *Mausi*! The day the idols will be made from the *Darus* and installed! That day, I will urinate on Kalapahada!
Old Woman	: Hey, my son, where will the idols be made?
Servitor-I	: In the courtyard of Gopal Jew Temple inside our Gajapati Maharaja's palace.

[Darus of Balabhadra, Jagannatha, Subhadra and Sudarshana have passed the gathering one after another on the road with the sounds of trumpet, and the chanting of 'Hari' name- Two persons of the crowd come forward. A song is heard on stage.]

Song	: In the world is One Brahma, no second; That *Darubrahma* you are, the soul-charioteer. You can't be drowned in water; you can't be burnt in fire, The swords can't chop you; you live forever. When you want, you change your body, *Nabakalebara, Nabakalebara, Nabakalebara, Nabakalebara.*
Servitor-I	: Hey, bloody fellow! Why do you move fast? Stand there to give some space. Lamps are lit on the road, and Rangolis are drawn in rice powder. Can't you see?
Person	: I want to see!
Servitor	: You can't see standing on either side of

the road; you are coming to the front. If I give you a fist; you will be set right! Hey, Brothers! Chant the name of 'Hari'. *Daru* has come.

[All chant the name of 'Hari' and say 'Jay Jagannatha'- the Old Woman rolls on the ground.]

Old Woman : O, Kalia, now my life is blessed to see you- Having lost all my family members, I was alone. But I have never believed to visit you in Sri Mandir. Having seen the *Daru*, today I think- Nobody can ruin or destroy you.

"You do and help others do;
Nothing happens here without you."

[Light off]

SCENE-XXIII

[At Ramachandra's Court, Dana Patra stands hand-cuffed by a soldier, while on the other side, Bishar Mohanty stands. Ramachandra says, looking at them.]

Ramachandra : Since the rule of Kapilendra Deva, it was declared that Sri Jagannatha is the King of Utkal and the Gajapatis are His servants. That's why they sweep the chariots holding golden broomsticks in their hands during the holy *Rathayatra* (Chariot Festival). It is practised since then. Jagannatha is the soul of every Odia! Jagannatha is the bridge of his soul, political unity and integrity! But Dana Patra, because of your greed, you handed over Jagannatha to Kalapahada. You can't be forgiven for this crime. I declare the capital punishment for a traitor like you! After you, your younger brother Baghu Patra will be the headman of Kokalagada, and awarded the title 'Bahu Balendra'. Messenger, take Dana Patra from here!

[Rajguru and three servitors come to the stage.]

All	:	Let there be victory for Gajapati!
Servitor-I	:	Yes, that scoundrel should be cut into pieces. This man has sold Jagannatha!
Servitor-II	:	Leave him to me. Squeezing his throat, I will take a bloodbath here!
Servitor-III	:	O, stupid! Will you go to heaven with the lands? Nobody will live in your family to do your rituals, scoundrel!
Ramachandra	:	Please be silent! Messenger, take Dana Patra away from here!

[The Messenger drags Dana Patra from this place.]

Ramachandra	:	The Bishar Mohanty, who takes risks bringing Brahmas from the 'Land of Banga' and helps the idols of Jagannatha and three other deities install here, I like to award him with the title of the headman. To make this event memorable, I will donate three Brahman villages to him for his supervision!
Servitor-III	:	Let Jagannatha bless Bishar Karana!
Rajguru	:	His Majesty! The work is over after the installation of Brahmas in the newer idols. The idols are ready to be mounted on *Ratnavedi* in Sri Mandir. Then, the people will start visiting the '*Nabajauban Besha* of Lord Jagannatha'.
Servitor-I	:	Jagannatha was not in Sri Mandir for eight years. We were in trouble and perplexed in his absence!
Servitor-II	:	No pilgrims were seen at the Principal Gate. The temple was very dreary. Today, Jagannatha, being bejewelled, shines beautifully!

Servitor-I	:	Mahaprabhu has returned, Master!
Servitor-III	:	O, Brother; who is the master. The Master is in *Badadeula* (Sri Mandir). All said that Kalapahada took away Jagannatha. We couldn't see Jagannatha. But Maharaj, starting from the selection of *Daru* to the making of the idols and the installation of Brahmas in the idols were accomplished smoothly this year. We couldn't imagine!
Rajguru	:	These are Lord Jagannath's wishes! Please come, My Lord. All others await you at the temple to see the *'Nabajaubana Besha* of Jagannatha'.
Ramachandra	:	Let's move, Rajguru Sahib.

[All leave the place, and the stage is lit off.]

SCENE-XIV

[Ratnasinghasana (bejewelled throne) is made ready with the recitation of verses. In it are mounted the idols of Jagannatha, Balabhadra, Subhadra and Sudarshana. Two servitors stand aside. Umrao suddenly reaches there. Having seen him, the servitors have come forward.]

Servitor-I : Who are you here? What's your caste? What's your *gotra* (lineage)? How come you are here?

Umrao : My Lord, I don't know my lineage. I have come from the 'Land of Banga' to pay a visit to Lord Jagannatha.

Servitor-II : Nobody stops this man in the compound where the 'chanting of hymns in praise of Lord Jagannatha' is continued. He comes straight to the *garbhagriha* (sanctum sanctorum). With one blow your face will turn into an ugly monkey's.

Umrao : What's my crime?

Servitor-I : Again, you ask me what crime you have committed. He is lying. Did you say your lineage, when you entered the temple?

Umrao : I don't know my lineage. How can I tell you?

[At this time, Ramachandra Deva comes with Rajguru and Servitor-III.]

Servitor-III : Hey, Bisuni, what happened?
Servitor-I : O, Nana; come fast. He doesn't know his caste and lineage. He enters the temple. Now, Jagannatha will take a bath! We have to make the temple holy again! This scoundrel has defiled our visit to see the *'Nabajauban Besha* of Lord Jagannatha'.
Ramachandra : You have obstructed the rituals of Lord Jagannatha. Do you know what punishment you can be given for this?
Umrao : His Majesty! I have not committed any crime here. I have been invited by a Vaishnav Saint. So, I have come here to see Lord Jagannatha!
Ramachandra : Who is that Vaishnav Saint?

[At this moment, Bishar Mohanty enters the temple with an older woman.]

Bishar : Maharaj, I have invited him!

[All of them look at Bishar Mohanty.]

Bishar : He is Umrao! He hails from the third Hindu caste. After Kalapahada immersed the half-burnt idol of Jagannatha in the Ganga, I first jumped into it. But I couldn't find any trace of Him. After I wandered being agitated for six months, one day, I got information that this Umrao brought four half-burnt bodies or logs from the river bank of Ganga and stored them at his home, considering them as the firewood. Having reached him, I realized these half-burnt bodies were of our four

	deities. I collected Brahmas from them. In Umrao's orchard, we buried the half-burnt idols. I assured him that, if we installed Jagannatha in Sri Mandir again, I would help him see Jagannatha at Puri. Thus, he has not committed any crime; it's my fault. You can punish me!
Ramachandra :	Bishar Karan Saint! Before Jagannatha, all were equal, irrespective of caste, creed, and colour. He has extended his vast arms to embrace the distressed and the fallen. He is above caste, creed and colour. That's why he comes to Umrao's house! To him, there is no distinction between the King and the ordinary man. Umrao has no fault here. He loves Jagannatha. Therefore, at this auspicious moment of *Nabakalebara*, let's come together to pray to Lord Jagannatha!
Old Woman :	Hey *Patitapabana* (God of the distressed and the fallen), Mahaprabhu! My eyes are made holy today. May your flag of glory flutter forever, Lord Jagannatha!

[Nabakalebara song is heard inside, and the play ends here.]

Song :	See how beautiful *Nabakalebara*, *Nabajauban Besha* of Lord Jagannatha is! Sins of a thousand births will vanish. On the bejewelled throne, the four idols Look very attractive and eye-catching, Everywhere is heard 'Jay Jay Jagannatha'. Here is a crowd of devotees, open for the public to see the mystery of Lord Jagannatha.

See, thirty-three crores of deities showered flowers from heaven,
Seeing the beauty of Sri Jagannatha, the creation is blessed today.
Who can fathom your wish to take new forms,
Nabakalebara, Nabakalebara, Nabakalebara, Nabakalebara!

>   *[Light off]*
>   *[END]*

Glossary of Terms

1. *Nabakalebara* : Brahma (Soul) remains unaltered and gets installed in newer forms, while the Darus (wooden bodies) of Jagannath and other deities are changed.
2. *Gahana Bije* : A special visit of the Queen to Jagannath Temple, Puri with special security forces
3. *Virashree Gajapati Goudeshwar* : The titles of the King of Kalinga after winning different regions
4. *Nabakoti Karnat Kalabargeswar Viradhi Virabar* : The titles of the King of Kalinga after winning different regions
5. *Srikshetra* : Puri, the place of Jagannatha Temple
6. *Patitapabana* : Jagannatha is of the distressed and the sinful
7. *Gajapati* : The King of Puri
8. *Mahaprabhu* : Jagannatha
9. *Darubrahma* : Jagannatha, Balabhadra, Subhadra and Sudarshana
10. *Mahaprasad* : Cooked food offered to Lord

		Jagannatha
11.	*Naibedya*	: Offerings of fruits or eatables to deities
12.	*Bhabagrahi*	: Jagannatha who understands our senses and feelings well.
13.	*Abhada*	: Offerings made to Lord Jagannatha
14.	*Singhadwar*	: Principal Door of Jagannatha Temple
15.	*Ratnasighasana*	: Bejewelled Throne
16.	*Ratnavedi*	: Bejewelled Throne
17.	*Daruvigrah*	: Idol
18.	*Banajaga jatra*	: *Night-awake Journey for identifying sacred Neem trees for Idols*
19.	*Darubruksha*	: *Neem trees selected for the Idols of Jagannatha and other deities*
20.	*Daru*	: *Cut-down Neem trees loaded on bullock carts to Jagannatha Temple or Sacred Neem trees or woods*
21.	*Rathayatra*	: *Chariot Festival*
22.	*Nabajauban Besha*	: *New Youth Get-up or Form of Lord Jagannatha*
23.	*Badadeula*	: *Jagannatha Temple*
24.	*Garbhagriha*	: *Sanctum Sanctorum*
25.	*Khuda*	: *Fragments of grains of rice*
26.	*Goudadesh*	: *Land of Goudas*

Black Eagle Books

www.blackeaglebooks.org
info@blackeaglebooks.org

Black Eagle Books, an independent publisher, was founded as a nonprofit organization in April, 2019. It is our mission to connect and engage the Indian diaspora and the world at large with the best of works of world literature published on a collaborative platform, with special emphasis on foregrounding Contemporary Classics and New Writing.

www.ingramcontent.com/pod-product-compliance
Lightning Source LLC
Chambersburg PA
CBHW060618080526
44585CB00013B/888